A Woman Of Joy

A BIBLE STUDY FOR WOMEN

A Woman Of
JOY

8 Studies from 1, 2, and 3 John

Dee Brestin

ChariotVICTOR
PUBLISHING
A DIVISION OF COOK COMMUNICATIONS

OTHER TITLES BY DEE BRESTIN

The Joy of Hospitality (Victor)
The Joy of Eating Right (Victor)
The Joy of Women's Friendships (Victor)
A Woman of Value (Victor)
A Woman of Insight (Victor)
A Woman of Joy (Victor)
The Friendships of Women Workbook (Victor)
We Are Sisters (Victor)

Fisherman Bible Studyguides (Shaw)
Proverbs and Parables
Examining the Claims of Christ (John 1-5)
1, 2 Peter and Jude
How Should a Christian Live? (1, 2, 3 John)
Higher Ground
Building Your House on the Lord: Marriage and Parenthood
Friendship: Portraits from God's Family Album

Most Scripture quotations are from the *Holy Bible: New International Version*®. Copyright © 1973, 1978, 1984 by International Bible Society. Used by permission of Zondervan Publishing House. All rights reserved; other Scriptures are taken from (TLB) *The Living Bible*, © 1971, Tyndale House Publishers, Wheaton, IL 60189. Used by permission; (KJV) *King James Version*; (TM) *The Message*. Copyright ©1993. Used by permission of NavPress Publishing House.

Editor: Pamela T. Campbell
Cover Design: Andrea Boven
Cover Photo: Brian MacDonald

Recommended Dewey Decimal Classification: 227.94
Suggested Subject Heading: NT: 1, 2, 3 JOHN
© 1995 by Dee Brestin.

11 12 13 14 Printing/Year 05 04 03 02

Victor Books is an imprint of ChariotVictor Publishing,
a division of Cook Communications, Colorado Springs, Colorado 80918
Cook Communications, Paris, Ontario
Kingsway Communications, Eastbourne, England

Contents

Introduction

Having been involved in women's Bible studies for thirty years, I was excited to write a guide specifically for women based on John's letters. While John was writing to all believers, his themes are of particular interest to women.

The first and prevailing theme is love. John wants us to love Jesus and each other—so that our joy will be complete! (1 John 1:4) You will be encouraged to open your heart to your sisters in Christ, to bond together, and to answer many "heart" as well as "head" questions. I am praying your love for one another will grow by leaps and bounds!

Another prevailing theme in the letters of John is confidence. Many women struggle with feelings of inadequacy. John will show us how our confidence can grow in our salvation, in our identity as God's children, and in our prospects of facing Jesus unashamed at His return. As our confidence grows, so will our joy.

Other themes that most women find applicable include helping our children walk in the truth and developing the art of hospitality.

To get the most out of this study:

1. Do your homework! For your convenience, each lesson is divided into five quiet times for your daily devotions.

2. Mark the questions where you would like to share in discussion—then take courage and speak up! If you are naturally talkative, don't star more than three questions. (The shyer women *need* silent spaces to speak up!)

3. Look over the material at the end of this guide. In addition to leader's notes on specific questions, you will find memory verses, songs that correlate with John's letters, and prayer sheets.

May John's letters impact your life and cause your joy to be full!

One

The Joy of the Fellowship Circle

1 John 1:1-4

Fellowship with Jesus
Fellowship with believers

My first remembrance of an awareness of God occurred when I was about three years old. Alone in my father's library, whirling around and waving my hands dramatically to Beethoven's Fifth, I suddenly had a profound question. "Who made my hands?" Just as quickly, the answer came. "God made your hands." God!

My first awareness of Jesus came, I believe, though Christmas and its carols. On Christmas Eve at a candlelight service, we sang: "O Holy Night" and I thought, *This really happened—the baby, the star, the shepherds. . . . Wow! Jesus!*

But it wasn't until I was a young wife and mother that I understood that Jesus and God were One. My older sister Sally explained the claims of Christ to me, and urged me to give my life to Him. Sally said:

> Dee, do you know who the Bible says Jesus is? The Bible says He is God! John tells us that Jesus was there with God "in the beginning" and that *He was God,* and that "all things were made by Him" (John 1:1-3). Jesus didn't begin at Christmas. He has always been! In the mystery of the Trinity, Jesus is the Creator! And though He made the universe, He loved you enough, Dee, to die for you to pay for your sin. And He wants you to give Him your whole life.

Jesus was God, and Jesus was interested in me personally. Oh, the wonder of it all.

The beginning of true joy—of a joy that cannot pass away—is the understanding of who Jesus is. Trusting Him and experiencing fellowship with Him is the most important secret of life, and that is what John is brimming to tell us—not only in the first chapter of his Gospel, but here again, in the beginning of his letters. His wonder, his excitement, at having actually been with Jesus, of touching Him, of seeing Him with his own eyes—brims up and overflows through the pages and down to us today.

And the second joy is connected to the first—the joy of Christian fellowship. A vital relationship with the living Lord has a direct impact on the quality of your fellowship with other believers. Being together with those who know Jesus personally, and who are retaining the wonder of it all, is akin to putting two smoldering logs together—suddenly, they burst into flame!

And finally, the circle should come back to the beginning, to fellowship with Jesus. When some believers get together, they do not habitually bring one another back to Jesus. But in spiritually mature friendships, their conversation brings their thoughts back to Jesus.

The first Letter of John shows us the circle of fellowship: fellowship with Jesus which leads to fellowship with one another, which leads back to fellowship with Jesus.

OPENING SONG
John's letters have inspired many praise choruses. Today learn "This Is My Commandment" (p. 96) and "Beloved (1 John 4:7-8)" (p. 95).

WARMUP
Read over the introduction together and then have each woman share her name, a little about herself, and why she came to this study.

Have each woman share an early memory of her awareness of the wonder of God or of Jesus.

MEMORY VERSE

We proclaim to you what we have seen and heard, so that you also may have fellowship with us. And our fellowship is with the Father and with His Son, Jesus Christ. We write this to make our joy complete (1 John 1:3-4).

SCRIPTURE STUDY

The Scripture study is divided into five days, for five personal quiet times with the Lord.

DAY 1

Background

Imagine the setting. John the Apostle, the youngest disciple whom, according to history, outlived all the others, is an old man now writing tenderly to the family of God. He was with Jesus — he "beheld His glory" (John 1:14), he laid his head on Jesus' breast, he ran to the empty tomb on Easter morning, and he was with the resurrected Christ when Jesus appeared and asked His disciples to touch Him, for "a ghost does not have flesh and bones, as you see I have" (Luke 24:39b).

John was there at Pentecost, when tongues of fire came down, and played an integral part in the spread of the early church. But now Christianity has been around for a while and many are second or even third generation Christians. William Barclay writes:

In the first days of Christianity there was a glory and a splendour, but now Christianity has become a thing of habit, "traditional, half-hearted, nominal." Men had grown used to it and something of the wonder was lost. . . . John was writing at a time when, for some at least, the first thrill was gone and the flame of devotion had died to a flicker (*The Letters of John and Jude*, Westminster Press, p. 3).

This letter was written from Ephesus, the same church that John gives a message to in Revelation. As you read this message you can see John's concern for the family of God. And how true this concern is today as well, for we too are in danger of losing our first love!

11

Read Revelation 2:1-7.

1. What are some of the things for which Jesus praises the people of the Ephesian church in verses 2-3?

2. What does Jesus hold against them? (v. 4) What does this mean?

J.B. Phillips paraphrases verse 4: "You do not love as you did at first."

Can you remember how you loved Jesus when you first came to know Him? Describe what you were like.

3. Jesus tells the church at Ephesus to do three things in order to return to the love that they originally had for Him. What are they? (v. 5)

One of the things that we see throughout the letters of John is that our relationship with God affects our relationship with each other. If our relationship with God is strong, then we will have the power to forgive and to love each other with the kind of love that does not give up. But if our relationship with God has lost its "first-love fervor," then our love may fail when it faces a test.

4. As you think about the steps that Jesus gave for restoring first love for Him, how might you put them into practice with a relationship in your family or in the family of God that is not what you would like it to be?

DAY 2

We Saw Him! We Heard Him! We Touched Him!

Peter, James, and John were the three whom Jesus chose to take to the mountain where they had a glimpse, in the transfiguration, of His future glory. Again, Jesus chose these three to take to the Garden of Gethsemane, where they had a glimpse of His future suffering. Peter transports us across the centuries with his excitement, when he says:

> For we have not been telling you fairy tales when we explained to you the power of our Lord Jesus Christ and His coming again. My own eyes have seen His splendor and His glory (2 Peter 1:16, TLB).

And John, likewise, says:

> The Word became flesh and blood,
> and moved into the neighborhood.
> We saw the glory with our own eyes (John 1:14a, TM);

and,

> From the very first day, we were there, taking it all in—we heard it with our own ears, saw it with our own eyes, verified it with our own hands. The Word of Life appeared right before our eyes; we saw it happen! (1 John 1:1, TM)

5. What are Peter and John trying to communicate to us in the above passages?

6. Think of a time when you were acutely aware that Jesus was real—that He was, as Peter said, "no fairy tale," but that He really existed and truly cared about you.

As I was reading these wonderful words of John again, and sensing his wonder, the words to "The Wonder of It All" kept going through my mind. In your own quiet time, sing "The Wonder of It All" (p. 94).

7. John tells us in his Gospel that "though the world was made through Him, the world did not recognize Him" (John 1:10). What evidence do you see that the world does not recognize Jesus, who was from the beginning?

8. How do you imagine your life might be different if you did not know the One who is from the beginning?

9. Have you received new life and new power because of Jesus? If so, share, in a sentence, when this happened or when you were first aware of a difference in you because of Jesus.

Christianity is more than a religion, because every religion has one basic characteristic. Its followers are trying to reach God, find God, please God through their own efforts. Religions reach up toward God. Christianity is God reaching down to man. Christianity claims that men have not found God, but that God has found them (Fritz Ridenour, *How To Be A Christian Without Being Religious,* Regal, Introduction).

DAY 3
. . . .

The Joy of Fellowship with Other Believers

As baby Christians, my husband and I moved across the country where Steve began a ninety-hour-a-week internship at a Seattle Hospital. Alone with two toddlers and acutely missing friends and family in the Midwest, I timidly tried a "Young Mom's Bible Study Group." I listened silently, fearing that if I spoke, I would say something stupid! Yet I was intrigued at how relevant the Scriptures were to our lives as women, mothers, and wives — and the strength the women were finding from the Scripture. At the close, they went around the table taking prayer requests. When my turn came, I tried to summon the courage to tell them of my loneliness in this new city, but instead, I was overwhelmed by tears. I couldn't speak! I was so embarrassed to be crying in front of a group of strangers. But I will never forget their response, the kind of response that I now see is characteristic of those who have a strong relationship with Jesus. A few women came up and put their arms around me. A few more began to pray for me (without having a clue as to what was wrong!). And afterward, the invitations began to come: for lunch, for a walk around Green Lake with our children, and for a time of praying for our families. Oh, the sweetness of Christian fellowship! Those women threw me a lifeline that year — and helped me find strength in the One who is "from the beginning!"

10. If you are in a small group, how does it enrich your life?

Read 1 John 1:1-4.
11. According to this passage, describe Christian fellowship. How is it different, for example, from the kind of fellowship football fans experience?

The Message paraphrases 1 John 1:3-4 as:

> We saw it, we heard it, and now we're telling you so you can experience it along with us, this experience of communion with the Father and His Son, Jesus Christ. Our motive for writing is simply this: We want you to enjoy this, too. Your joy will double our joy!

12. Think about a time when your excitement about Jesus spread to someone else. Share what happened and how you felt.

The strength of Christian fellowship, whether it is in the home, a small group, or another setting, is dependent on the strength of each individual's fellowship with the Father and His Son, Jesus Christ. With that in mind, how can the individuals in this group help their fellowship be the best it can be?

15

How tepid is the love of so many who call themselves by His name. How tepid our own—my own—in comparison with the lava fires of His eternal love. I pray that you may be an ardent lover, the kind of lover who sets others on fire (Amy Carmichael, *Candles in the Dark*, Christian Literature Crusade, p. 107).

DAY 4
A Strong Group Does Not Neglect God's Word!

When doing a live radio interview on my series of Bible study guides for women, the interviewer tried to provoke a reaction from me with the following opener:

> Don't you think that women's Bible study groups are essentially coffee klatches? It seems to me they never accomplish much. They laugh together and cry together—but God's Word is neglected.

My response was:

> I *have* been in women's groups that are all heart and no head. But I have also experienced male leadership that neglects the needs of people.

> "For instance?" my interviewer queried.

> I remember visiting a Sunday school class led by a man when I was new in a church. I was not introduced to the class, nor was there any class interaction. He covered his ten points, but I left feeling lonelier than when I came—and I didn't go back.

> "I see," my interviewer conceded, graciously. "Christian fellowship needs to be a balance between head and heart—between a study of God's Word and ministering to the individuals."

Precisely! Women must not neglect the lesson, and men must not neglect the people. The First letter of John clarifies that the best fellowship begins with God and then fans out to embrace individuals. Then those individuals bring one another back to God.

13. In order to keep this group from being a coffee klatch, it is vital to focus on God and His Word, to find ways to sharpen one another, and to keep the wonder of the reality of Jesus alive. The following are Scriptural ways to do that. Write down what you learn from each passage and how you might practice this truth in this group (or, if you are doing this study as an individual, how to do it in your family or other groups of believers).

A. Let the word of Christ dwell in you richly as you teach and admonish one another with all wisdom (Col. 3:16a).

B. and as you sing psalms, hymns and spiritual songs with gratitude in your hearts to God (Col. 3:16b).

14. What can your group do to avoid becoming a coffee klatch?

DAY 5

A Strong Group Does Not Neglect Its Members!

First John 3:13 shows that true fellowship begins with God, fans out and embraces each other, and helps each other come back to God. It's a circle:

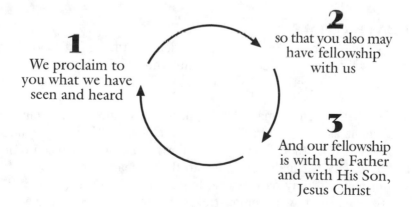

1
We proclaim to you what we have seen and heard

2
so that you also may have fellowship with us

3
And our fellowship is with the Father and with His Son, Jesus Christ

15. Describe how a Bible study group (or Christian family or two women friends) might accomplish this circle.

16. The following are Scriptural admonitions warning us not to neglect the needs of one another. Write down what you learn from each passage and how you might practice this truth in your group (or, if you are doing this study as an individual, how to do it in your family or other groups of believers).

    A. Greet one another with a holy kiss (1 Cor. 16:20)

    B. Therefore encourage one another and build each other up (1 Thes. 5:11).

    C. The purposes of a man's heart are deep waters, but a man of understanding draws them out (Prov. 20:5a).

    D. Therefore confess your sins to each other and pray for each other so that you may be healed (James 5:16a).

17. What can your group members do to make each other feel loved and cared for?

PRAYER TIME

Many people are intimidated by the idea of praying out loud. This guide will be gentle, leading you into this gradually. And no one will ever be forced to pray out loud.

Today, have each woman share a personal request. For example, she might ask, "I would like to grow closer to God" or "I need wisdom as a mother." Write these down, and pray for each other at home. Pay particular attention to the woman on your right, for whom you will pray daily. Close by singing "Beloved (1 John 4:7-8)" (p. 95). See how it demonstrates the circle that this lesson has been talking about!

Two

The Joy of Walking in the Light
1 John 1:5–2:11

Our eighteen-year-old daughter Sally tells of going to a youth conference where she was told.

When God speaks to you and you shut Him out, a callous forms on your heart—and the next time, it's harder to hear Him.

Last summer Sally was in a movie theatre when she heard God speak to her. She tells the story:

I was eating popcorn and thoroughly enjoying this really cute movie. But about halfway through, suddenly a scene came where one of the characters was saying terrible things about Jesus. I became very uncomfortable. I thought, *I hope this scene passes quickly so I can enjoy the movie again.* And then I heard it. It wasn't an audible voice, but it was an impression on my heart that was so strong that I knew it was from the Lord. Only two words. *Just go.*

My first reaction was—*No way! I spent $5 and I'm enjoying this. I haven't been to a movie in forever!* But then I heard it again.

Just go.

I thought, *OK, Lord*. I leaned over to my brother and his girlfriend and I said, "J.R., let's just go."

And J.R. and his girlfriend looked at each other and I could tell they were going through exactly the same struggle I had just been through—the struggle to obey God's voice. They both hesitated and then looked thoughtfully at the screen.

More blasphemy! Suddenly they agreed: "OK! Let's go!" The three of us got up and walked out of the theatre, and it felt so good to know we had heard *and* obeyed!

In his letter, John uses the analogy of fellowship with God as living in the light. If you want to have fellowship with God, you stay in the light. As soon as you walk into darkness, you cut off your fellowship (not your relationship) with God, for God cannot go into darkness. To resume fellowship, you must confess your sin and return to the light. If you refuse, you will walk further and further into the darkness, until the darkness blinds you.

OPENING SONG

Sing "Beloved (1 John 4:7-8)" (p. 95) and "Father, I Adore You" (p. 93). Both can be sung in rounds. Also learn and sing "If We Walk In The Light" (p. 98).

WARMUP

Share a recent time when you heard God speak to you—either through His Word, through another believer, or through His still, small voice. Share your response and how it made you feel.

MEMORY VERSE

But if we walk in the light, as He is in the light, we have fellowship with one another, and the blood of Jesus, His Son, purifies us from all sin (1 John 1:7).

SCRIPTURE STUDY

The Scripture study is divided into five days, for five personal quiet times with the Lord.

DAY 1

God Is Light!

While on a ski vacation as a little girl I attended an Easter Sunrise Service on top of a mountain in Aspen, Colorado. At 5:45 A.M., snow crunched under our boots as my family headed in the darkness to board the chairlift. As we ascended, we gazed in wonder at the stars above us. We pulled our blankets tightly around us as thin protection from the strong wind which whistled through the pines and straight to our bones.

At the top we joined a growing crowd seated at picnic tables facing east. The panoramic sky grew lighter as we waited in hushed anticipation. Suddenly the bright red rim of the sun peeked from behind a lower mountain range. Slowly, surely, it flooded the sky with radiant splendor and our bodies with welcome warmth. Some enthusiastic young men with guitars led us in "Christ the Lord Is Risen Today!" and "Up from the Grave He Arose!" In the glory of that service, our cold chairlift ride was forgotten. Thinking back to that time today, I am reminded of Isaiah's prophecy:

> The people walking in darkness have seen a great light; on those living in the land of the shadow of death, a light has dawned (Isa. 9:2).

Read 1 John 1:5-7.

1. What do we learn about God in verse 5? What are some of the characteristics of light?

Betsie ten Boom, who died in a Nazi concentration camp, urged her sister Corrie to get the message out: "We must tell people what we have learned . . . that no darkness can keep out God's marvelous light. They will believe us, because we've been there" (Joan Brown, *Corrie: The Lives She's Touched,* Revell, p. 72).

2. Throughout Scripture, God is associated with light. In each of the following, explain why you think the metaphor of light is used.

21

A. The Lord is my light and my salvation, whom shall I fear? The Lord is the stronghold of my life—of whom shall I be afraid? (Ps. 27:1)

B. Praise be to the name of God for ever and ever; wisdom and power are His . . . He reveals deep and hidden things; He knows what lies in darkness, and light dwells with him (Dan. 2:20, 22).

Read 1 John 1:5-7 again.
3. How does the truth of verse 5 lead to the conclusion of verse 6?

Share a time when you were aware of losing fellowship with God because you had wandered into darkness.

If you get out of the light, you become a sentimental Christian, and live only on your memories, and your testimony will have a hard metallic ring to it. Beware of trying to cover up your present refusal to "walk in the light" by recalling your past experiences when you did "walk in the light" (Oswald Chambers, *My Utmost for His Highest,* Discovery House, 8/13).

DAY 2
Guarding Our Homes Against Darkness
In Titus 2:3-5, the older women are told to teach the younger women a number of things. One of them, as translated in the KJV, is to be "keepers at home." Literally, the Greek word *keepers* is derived from the word for "guard." A woman, therefore, who has a family, has a responsibility to guard her home against evil influences, against darkness. A Christian home should be one that is full of light, and which is not hospitable to the forces of darkness. (We will see this again in 2 John.)

4. Perhaps the most common conduit of darkness is the mass media. Not everything is dark, but much is. Have you found

some things that work which help you guard your home against the darkness of television?

Against the darkness of trashy novels, magazines, etc.?

Against the darkness of music with unholy lyrics?

When our sons were young, I did not screen the music that came into our home as I should have. I severely regret it — and both tell me the music had a very negative impact on them. Both went through a time when they were far from the Lord. Because of the Lord's mercy, they are both now walking closely with Him. However, with our next three children, who are all daughters, we are guarding our home against unholy music. Our daughter Sally says: "It helped my thought life tremendously to be exposed only to Christian or edifying music."

Read 1 John 1:7-9.
5. We also have a responsibility as mothers (or as mentors) to help our children learn how to walk in the light and learn what to do the moment they realize they have wandered into darkness. What should we train them to do and why?

In *First We Have Coffee* (Here's Life, p. 40), Margaret Jensen describes her childhood bedtime ritual with her mother:

> Every detail of school and play came up on the bedtime screen. Nothing was hidden from Mama. As she tucked me in, she always said, "Look at me, Margaret. Is there anything you need to tell me before we talk to God?" Knowing her secret line to God, the confession poured out, and forgiveness followed. Sleep was sweet.

6. First John 2:9 says: "Anyone who claims to live in God's light and hates a brother or sister is still in the dark" (TM). As a mother, can you share any practical hints on:

23

A. Reducing sibling rivalry?

B. Training your children to treat one another with kindness?

C. Helping your children have warm, enjoyable times together?

DAY 3 . . . .

Recognizing and Dealing with Our Sinful Nature

According to 1 John 1:10, you are either a sinner or a liar! Every single individual has a sin nature, and our hearts, Jeremiah tells us, "are desperately wicked" (Jer. 17:9).

Read 1 John 1:8-10.
7. What do verses 8 and 10 tell us about human nature?

Sin, in the Greek, means "missing the mark." Every single one of us has fallen short of the holiness of God.

Reluctance to admit wrongdoing affects our relationship with God—and with others. Once, when speaking at a conference about the sins that hurt our friendships, I mentioned laziness. A young woman came up to me afterward and told me the following story:

> Two years ago my closest woman friend moved away—for a year. We promised to write during that year apart. However—I didn't. The reason I gave her when she moved back was that I'd had a baby and had been so busy. However, when I tried to resume our friendship—I ran up against a wall!

> Tonight, when you talked about the sin of laziness, the Holy Spirit convicted me. My friend was here, so right afterward I went over to her and said: "The reason I didn't write wasn't because I was too busy, but because I was too lazy! I didn't

24

see that until tonight. I was wrong and I'm so sorry I hurt you. I miss you so much. Will you forgive me?" We both started to cry and flung our arms around each other. The wall came tumbling down!

Just as confession can restore fellowship with a friend, so can it restore fellowship with God.

Personal Prayer Time
In your individual quiet time, right now, take a moment for praise and confession.

Praise
1. Praise God for a fear He has delivered you from — because He is light.
2. Praise God for guidance He has given you — because He is light.

Confession
David came to God in order to be searched by the Light. He prayed: "Search me, O God, and know my heart; test me and know my anxious thoughts. See if there is any offensive way in me, and lead me in the way everlasting" (Ps. 139:23-24).

1. Pray this prayer and be still before God.
2. Confess and turn from anything He sheds light on.

DAY 4
A Child of the Light Is Obedient
I see her in the mirror — I hear her in the things I say. I am becoming my mother! People recognize her in me and comment on it. Likewise, because I am a child of God, I should reflect some of His characteristics as well. This is a central theme of 1 John. If we are truly born of God, we will be like Him. Here, the characteristic that John stresses is obedience. Jesus was completely obedient. If we have Jesus in us, there should be obedience in our lives. (The obedience will not be perfect, as 1 John 1:8 makes clear, but it should be characteristic, for children reflect their parents.)

Read 1 John 2:1-2.
8. What is God's best for us, according to 1 John 1:2a? And what is His second best according to 1 John 2:2b?

It's always better not to sin. It is better, for example, to abstain from sexual intimacy before marriage. Studies show those who do have better marriages and more fulfilling sexual relationships. However, if we do fall, full forgiveness is possible. Full forgiveness means we are clean in God's sight and that fellowship with Him is completely restored—but it doesn't mean that we will not reap the consequences of our actions.

9. John says, "I write this to you so that you will not sin." What are some areas where, if you refuse to sin, you will experience more joy and peace?

10. How is Jesus described in verses 1-2?

Read 1 John 2:3-6.
11. What should be characteristic of the woman who says she knows God? Why? What does obedience lead to? Have you experienced this? If so, share a specific instance.

DAY 5
A Child of the Light Loves Her Sister (and Her Brother!)
When we adopted Annie, a five year old from an orphanage in Seoul, she was withdrawn and unresponsive. Yet God provided a six-year-old friend for Annie who reflected God's marvelous light and love. I'll never forget the day they met. Sarena placed a teddy-bear in Annie's arms. Annie threw that teddy-bear to the ground.

Sarena reached out for Annie's hand. Annie jerked her hand away. Sarena said, "Annie—I just want to be your friend!" Annie didn't understand English, and she scowled at Sarena.

I fully expected Sarena to give up. The most natural response in the world to pain and rejection is withdrawal. But Sarena didn't respond naturally, she responded supernaturally. She turned to me and said, "I don't care how long it takes, Mrs. Brestin. I am just going to keep on being nice to Annie—and one day we are going to be best friends." In time, God's marvelous light shone through Sarena to thaw the frozen heart of our little Annie.

Read 1 John 2:7-11.

12. What should be characteristic of the woman who claims to be in the light? Why?

    What happens to the woman who loves her sister?

    What happens to the woman who hates her sister?

13. Jesus said it was easy to love those who love us (even unbelievers, He said, do that.) The test is to love those who, for whatever reason, are hard to love. Is there someone who is hard to love in your life right now? How do you think God would have you respond to her (or him?)

14. When you are clean before the Lord, nothing is between you and the Light! When this is true, exciting things will be happening. The Light may give you guidance in an area where you need it; may answer a prayer; may thaw a frozen relationship; or may simply warm you with the joy of His presence. Share one way that you have experienced the joy of being in the Light recently.

15. What do you expect to remember from this lesson or the discussion of this lesson?

PRAYER TIME

An unintimidating form of group prayer is "Conversational Prayer," also called "Popcorn Prayer." The leader introduces a subject, or the name of a group member, and then as many women as wish offer a simple sentence. Then, when the "popping" stops, the leader lifts up the name of another group member. Take prayer requests. Then pray, using Popcorn Prayer. Close by singing "Beloved (1 John 4:7-8)" (p. 95).

POPCORN PRAYER

1. Introduce one person or subject at a time.
2. Prayers should be short "pops" from anyone anywhere in the circle.
3. Continue until "popping" stops.
4. Introduce another person or subject.

Three

The Joy That
Will Not Pass Away

1 John 2:12-29

There's a radiance that comes from within a woman who knows what brings lasting joy. She will risk everything for what is eternal and true, and even in the bleakest circumstances, experience joy.

Corrie ten Boom and her family fought against the lies of Hitler, risking their lives in order to hide Jews in their home. The family was eventually caught and transported to a concentration camp.

One night Corrie climbed out of her barracks when she heard that 250 prisoners were being taken to an unknown destination — perhaps, to their death. In a place hidden from the guards, she whispered encouragement to each as they went by:

"Jesus is Victor!" I whispered.

"Oh, Corrie — how could you? Go back to your barracks!"

"Fear not. Only believe."

"Thank you, Corrie. God bless you."

"Underneath are the everlasting arms. Jesus has said, 'I am with you til the end of the world. Look to the Lord. He loves you. Jesus is Victor!"

Corrie said, "There was joy in my heart as the Holy Spirit gave me a short message for everyone that went through the gate" (Joan Brown, *Corrie: The Lives She's Touched*, Revell, pp. 60-61).

OPENING SONG
Teach the round, "Rejoice in the Lord Always" (p. 99). Also sing "This Is My Commandment" (p. 96).

WARMUP
Name one thing which has given you fleeting happiness and then explain why that happiness didn't last. Give each group member an opportunity to respond.

MEMORY VERSE

The world and its desires pass away, but the man who does the will of God lives forever (1 John 2:17).

SCRIPTURE STUDY
The Scripture study is divided into five days, for five personal quiet times with the Lord.

DAY 1
She Knows She Has Everything That Truly Matters
We will experience trouble in this world, and yet, we have everything that truly matters if we are abiding in Christ.

1. Even in a concentration camp, Corrie ten Boom had all that really mattered. What were some of the treasures that she and her family possessed?

   Better a little with the fear of the Lord than great wealth with turmoil. Better a meal of vegetables where there is love than a fattened calf with hatred (Prov. 15:16-17).

2. Have you experienced fighting on an expensive vacation or over a costly meal—or contentment over soup? Share something about it.

Read 1 John 2:12-14.

3. John writes to believers of three different categories. Who are they?

What are some of the eternal treasures that they possess, because of Christ?

4. Take a moment and list some of the eternal treasures that you have because of Christ.

DAY 2

She Doesn't Give Her Heart to the World

What drives you? When you wake up in the morning, what do you think about as you plan your day?

John addresses three worldly drives in this key passage:

(1) the cravings of sinful man ("the lust of the flesh," KJV). Are we driven by our flesh--by sex, alcohol, food, or pleasure in general?

(2) the lust of his eyes. Are we driven by our eyes—by TV, movies, or entertainment in general?

(3) the boasting of what he has and does ("the pride of life," KJV). Are we driven by our pride—to possess a beautiful home, wardrobe . . . or to achieve a high-status position?

Read 1 John 2:15-17.

5. Each of us struggles with being dominated by the desires of the world. Ask the Lord to show you what, specifically, in each of the following areas, could easily dominate you—or perhaps *is* dominating you.

A. The lust of the flesh

B. The lust of the eyes

C. The pride of life

6. What reasons can you find in this passage for not giving your heart to the world?

On-the-Spot Action Assignment. Women are often gifted at making themselves vulnerable. This can lead to great healing. In this Action Assignment, you must determine to keep confidences. What is confessed in prayer *must not* be mentioned outside the group.

Ask three women to read the following parts of Anne, Lisa, and Judy.

Judy: "Lord, help me with my addiction to soap operas."
Anne: "Yes, Lord. Please help Judy."
Lisa: "Please help her fill that void with Christian radio or something she will enjoy yet will be pleasing to you."

Lisa: "Lord, please help me with my desire to be in the limelight, with my envy of the soloists in choir."
Judy: "Thank you for Lisa's honesty, Lord. Please help her and bless her."
Anne: "I agree, Lord."

Now break into groups of three and do likewise. Ask each woman to confess, audibly, one area that could or does have a stranglehold on her life. Then the other two will support her in prayer. Don't talk before or after you pray—just pray! And when God brings either of these women to your mind during the week, pray for them.

DAY 3 . . . .
She Fills Her Life with Things That Won't Pass Away
For those of you who have studied *A Woman of Insight,* you know how Solomon tried to bring meaning to his life with things that will

pass away: entertainment, beautiful homes, sex, and status. Each of these things brought him some fleeting pleasure, but at the end of the day, when he turned to consider what his life was really accomplishing, he said: "Everything was meaningless, a chasing after the wind; nothing was gained under the sun" (Ecc. 2:11b).

7. List some examples in your life of endeavors that brought fleeting pleasure but no lasting joy or meaning.

Often we fill our leisure time with TV or trips to the mall because we have formed bad habits. In order to break those habits, we must begin a new lifestyle. What are some ways you can spend your leisure time that would be helpful and lead to lasting joy?

In our laziness, we sometimes allow our children to watch too much TV or to play with toys that cause them to be preoccupied with violence or mature subjects (Barbies, video games, toy weapons, make up). In order to help our them break those habits, we must be creatively diligent. What are some ways you can help your children to change their lifestyle so that they too can experience the joy that will not pass away?

Entertainment is the devil's substitute for joy (Revivalist Leonard Ravenhill).

DAY 4 . . . .
She Discerns Error
In John's day, there were those who were infiltrating and offering a "new and improved" Christianity. The same is true today. We need to cling to the original teaching and continually check the things that we hear and read with the Word of God, to see if they are true.

Hitler claimed a mandate from God in his persecution of the Jews, but the ten Booms, because they were walking closely with God and knew His Word, easily recognized the lie. Today many who claim Christianity are at cross-purposes with the Gospel of Christ. John tells us how we can be protected against deceivers.

Read 1 John 2:18-20.
  8. What time does John say it is — and what does that mean?

Who is coming? And who will precede Him?

Then, as now, deniers of the Son called themselves Christians. What evidence does John give to show that they were never really part of the body of Christ?

Read 1 John 2:20-27.
  9. How does John reassure believers in verses 20 and 27? In 21?

10. What is the ultimate lie according to verse 22?

The words *Jesus* and *Christ* here are crucial. Kenneth Wuest explains that *Jesus* means "Jehovah saves" and contains the doctrine of the substitutionary atonement offered on the cross. *Christ* means "the anointed one," the "Messiah." "The denial therefore is that the person called Jesus was neither God nor man, and that on the Cross He did not offer an atonement for sin. Present day Modernism denies the deity of Jesus of Nazareth and the substitutionary atonement He offered on the cross, while subscribing to His humanity" (Kenneth Wuest, *Word Studies in the New Testament,* Eerdmans, pp. 134–35).

11. The lie in 1 John 2:22 is central, but John gives several other clues to help us discern false teachers. Find the warning sign in each of the following:

    A. 1 John 2:4

B. 1 John 2:9

C. 1 John 2:15

D. 1 John 2:19

E. 1 John 2:22

F. 1 John 2:23

G. 1 John 3:10

DAY 5
She Will Be Glad, Not Ashamed, When Jesus Comes Back

Pam and I sat on the dock dangling our feet into the waters of Lake Oswego on an Indian summer day. Pam was a new Christian and was telling me that this new life she had received had some surprises! Intently, she said:

"The first big surprise that Scripture revealed was that I was supposed to submit to my husband!"

I laughed. "What else has surprised you?"

Pam made a circle in the water with her foot. "You know what really blows me away?"

"Tell me!"

"That Jesus is coming back! I grew up in church—but I was never told that Jesus is coming back. Yet it's everywhere in the Scriptures! It gives me goosebumps to think about it, Dee. I want to be ready for Him. I don't want to be ashamed when He appears."

35

Remember that Jesus is coming back, and that it could be at any moment. Billy Graham has said that there are no more prophecies that need to be fulfilled before Jesus' return. This should inspire us to keep our eyes focused on heavenly things, not on the things that pass away, and to so abide in Christ that when that great day comes, we will be confident and ready.

12. What do you learn about Jesus' return from the following passages?

A. They were looking intently up into the sky as He was going, when suddenly two men dressed in white stood beside them. "Men of Galilee," they said, "why do you stand here looking into the sky? This same Jesus, who has been taken from you into heaven, will come back in the same way you have seen Him go into heaven" (Acts 1:10-11).

B. For the Lord Himself will come down from heaven, with a loud command, with the voice of the archangel and with the trumpet call of God, and the dead in Christ will rise first. After that, we who are still alive and are left will be caught up together with them in the clouds to meet the Lord in the air. And so we will be there with the Lord forever (1 Thes. 4:16-17).

C. Live deeply in Christ. Then we'll be ready for Him when He appears, ready to receive Him with open arms, with no cause for red-faced guilt or lame excuses when He arrives (1 John 2:28, TM).

13. When did you first realize Jesus was coming back?

How does this truth impact your daily life?

14. As you look over the first two chapters of 1 John, what kind of behavior is necessary in order for you to be unashamed when Jesus comes back?

    A. 1 John 1:7

    B. 1 John 1:9

    C. 1 John 2:3

    D. 1 John 2:6

    E. 1 John 2:10

    F. 1 John 2:15-17

    G. 1 John 2:28

15. Did you see any of the above characteristics in the ten Boom family?

    How is God speaking to you through this lesson?

On-the-Spot Action Assignment. Pass around a hat for women to put their names in to exchange secret sisters. Be faithful to pray for your secret sister and to show her love (such as encouraging notes, a loaf of homemade bread, or a bunch of wildflowers delivered by a co-conspirator!). You'll reveal your secret sisters the last week.

PRAYER TIME
Pray, using Popcorn Prayer. Close by singing "Rejoice in the Lord Always" (p. 99).

Four

The Joy of Calvary Love
1 John 3

As women, most of us have been gifted, by our Creator, to be nurturing. It's usually women who remember birthdays, organize family reunions, and respond to friends in pain with sympathetic tears. Even women who don't know the Lord often demonstrate this kind of love to their friends and family.

The difference I have seen in a woman who is abiding in Christ is that her love goes beyond a human response to a supernatural response. Like Christ, she responds to unkindness with kindness; she loves not just those who love her, but those who are hard to love; and she's alert, looking for ways to minister to those who are in spiritual, physical, or emotional need. Lee Ezell tells of just such a woman who ministered to her during the darkest hour of Lee's life.

Mom Croft spotted Lee visiting her church. Lee was pregnant, carrying a child conceived in rape. After her pregnancy was discovered, Lee's mother cast her out of their home. Lonely and desperate, Lee tells of meeting Mom Croft.

> After the service a great big woman with an equally big smile greeted me and said, "Where are you going to lunch, girl?" Lee followed Mom Croft and her husband to a tiny house just a half a block from the church.

"Just moved here, didn't you?" she said as she started cooking eggs, grits, and biscuits.

"Yes, how did you know?"

"I can tell," she said with a twinkle in her eye. "Mom Croft can spot a lonely, hungry girl."

Lee moved in with the Crofts (who in their tiny house always found room for a "stray"). Because of Mom Croft's Christlike love, Lee experienced great healing and found the spiritual courage to carry her baby to term and to give her daughter to a loving Christian couple (*The Missing Piece*, Bantam, p. 50).

The third chapter of 1 John begins with the wonderful phrase "Behold, what manner of love the Father has given unto us!" (KJV) In the Greek, "what manner of" is *potapen*, which means "what country, race or tribe?" It speaks of something foreign. It is not a natural kind of love—but a supernatural. And those who are born of God, who have Him in them, should be habitually exhibiting this same kind of foreign supernatural love to others. Mom Croft did it—and so can we—if we are abiding in Christ.

OPENING SONG
Teach "Behold, What Manner of Love" (p. 100) to your small group. Then sing "This Is My Commandment" (p. 96).

WARMUP
Share a time when someone was alert to your spiritual, emotional, or physical needs.

MEMORY VERSE

This is how we know what love is: Jesus Christ laid down his life for us. And we ought to lay down our lives for our brothers (1 John 3:16).

Most of you know John 3:16, so this should be an easy reference to remember!

SCRIPTURE STUDY

The Scripture study is divided into five days, for five personal quiet times with the Lord.

DAY 1 ....

She Rejoices in the "Foreign" Love of God

When I was a baby Christian, my husband was transferred to another city. When I heard the news, I called my sister Sally, who had led me to the Lord. "We're moving," I wept. "I can't believe we are leaving Seattle."

"Dee," my sister asked, "where is your real home?"

"Seattle!"

"No, Dee, your real home is in heaven. You are just sojourning down here. With His amazing love, God has reached down and made you one of His children. And just as Jesus was a sojourner, an alien on earth, so are you. Set your mind on things above, for your real life is hidden with Christ in God. One day Jesus is coming back to take you home" (Col. 3:2-4).

As the third chapter of 1 John begins, John again is filled with awe at the amazing, "foreign" love of God. Then he proceeds to the mysterious thought that we are like this "foreign" God, if we have been born of Him. We need to remember this—that we are strangers on this earth, that our citizenship is in heaven, and that our actions and our love should be very different from those who are not children of God.

In your personal quiet time, sing "Behold, What Manner of Love" (p. 100), and then spend a few moments in praise to God for His amazing love for you.

Read 1 John 3:1-3.

1. In verse 1, what are some of the words or phrases which capture John's awe at the love of God?

The Greek captures the idea that this love is not natural or usual — but actually foreign. How is God's love different from the kind of love that non-Christians have?

Share a time when you were particularly aware of God's amazing love for you.

2. Just as God's love is a foreign kind of love, so are His children like "foreigners," people from another planet! Why is it that the people of the world fail to understand the people of God? (v. 1)

Read 1 Peter 2:9-12.
3. What similar thoughts do you see in this passage?

Though unbelievers may not understand believers, they will be drawn to God through the righteousness of believers. Was that true in your life? If so, share an example.

4. According to 1 John 3:2, what are we now?

When will our physical bodies be transformed?

But our citizenship is in heaven. And we eagerly await a Savior from there, the Lord Jesus Christ, who, by the power that enables Him to bring everything under IIis control, will transform our lowly bodies so that they will be like His glorious body (Phil. 3:20-21).

According to the Philippians passage, what will our bodies be like?

What impact should all of the above truths have on our behavior? (1 John 3:3) What does this mean?

DAY 2
She Has the Very Nature of God
Read 1 John 3:4-10.

At first reading, this next section may surprise you. For John *seems* to say that the believer doesn't sin. However, that would not be consistent with 1 John 1:8. What he *is* saying is that if we have been born of God, we have God's nature. Therefore it would be inconsistent with the nature of God to be habitually turned toward sin the way an unbeliever is. The most accurate translations of verse 6 contain the concept of "continuing to sin."

5. In each of the following sections, state the two thoughts John links together (This is true, therefore this is also true):

   A. 1 John 3:5-6

   B. 1 John 3:7

   C. 1 John 3:8

   D. 1 John 3:9

6. What are two clear ways, according to verse 10, to discern who is a child of God and who is a child of the devil?

DAY 3
If We've Passed from Death to Life, We'll Love Each Other

In this fascinating section, John refers to Cain as an illustration of the truths he has been teaching.

Read Genesis 4:1-15.

7. Describe Cain's emotions in verse 5. Why do you think he was feeling this way?

What two alternatives did God say were before Cain — and with what resulting consequences?

Which did Cain choose, and what happened?

When our daughter Sally was twelve, we adopted an adorable five-year-old girl from an orphanage in Korea. Sally experienced some Cain-like sibling rivalry at that time, and now, at age eighteen, shares:

> I was excited about getting Annie — until she arrived. Then when I saw all the attention move from me to her, envy welled up in my heart. James 3:16 tells us that where you have envy, you find disorder and every evil practice. That envy led to my being unkind to Annie, and to a deep depression for me — sleepless nights and miserable days.
>
> At a Christian program one night the speaker talked about the importance of keeping Christ on the throne of our lives — and God convicted me that I had allowed myself to take over that throne. I went forward for a recommitment and asked God to take all the yuk I felt in my heart out, and to step back on the throne of my life. He filled me with a love for Annie. Today I cannot imagine life without Annie — I love her so much. And my heart is filled not only with love — but with joy!

8. Can you identify with the above story in any way?

Have you experienced disobedience leading to depression or obedience leading to joy? If so, share something about it.

Read 1 John 3:11-15.
9. What do you learn about Cain from this passage?

What point is John making with the story of Cain?

Is there an application for your life?

DAY 4
. . . .
She Will Not "Snap Shut Her Heart" To Brethren in Need

There have been times when God has brought "a sister in need" across my path and my honest thought is: *Lord, if I respond too warmly to her, I'll never be rid of her!* My natural response is to "snap shut my heart" or, as the *Scofield King James Version* translates it, "shutteth up his compassions."

Christ did not shut up His compassions from us—He died for us when we were helpless sinners. As children of God, we must not shut up our compassions from one another.

Read 1 John 3:16-18.

10. What example defines true love in verse 16? How could you apply this verse in your life right now? Be specific.

11. How does John exhort us to express Calvary love in verses 17-18?

12. Share a time when your natural response was to "snap shut your heart," or "shut up your compassions." Did you overcome that initial response or not? How did you then feel?

Jean Troup, the director of a shelter for homeless women in Maryland, shares her feelings in my book, *The Lifestyles of Christian Women* (Victor, pp. 133–34).

I think the Gospel demonstrates that God wants us to get involved with those in need because God could have just snapped His fingers and saved us, but instead He died on a cross. It always hurts to get involved, but I believe that is what He has called us to do. . . . The Lord has definitely converted me from a sheltered lifestyle to getting out and dealing with peoples' hurts and desperate situations from a faith perspective.

13. What hurting people are you aware of in your church, neighborhood, or life sphere?

Is God impressing a plan of action on your heart? If so, what?

DAY 5
A Habitually Loving Heart Is a Heart at Rest
In Amy Carmichael's book *If*, each page has a sentence describing Calvary love, such as:

If I fear to hold another to the highest because it is so much easier to avoid doing so, then I know nothing of Calvary love.

If I can enjoy a joke at the expense of another; if I can in any way slight another in conversation, or even in thought, then I know nothing of Calvary love.

Elisabeth Elliot said each sentence seared her, and each time the Holy Spirit said: "Guilty!" (*Bright Legacy*, Servant, p. 23)

That is the way each of us tends to feel after reading 1 John 3:16-18. We have fallen short of Calvary love. Our failures rise up, and our hearts condemn us! The solution to a condemning heart, John now tells us, has two parts:

1. Respond in repentance and find ways to actively love the hurting people God brings across your path. The result? Your heart will be set at rest in His presence!

2. But if you *still* have a condemning heart, realize that God is greater than your heart, and He will be more merciful toward you that you are toward yourself.

Read 1 John 3:18-24.

14. If we have received Jesus, then we have been born again. But sometimes our confidence can become shaky. What are some ways, according to the following verses, that you could set your heart at rest?

   A. 1 John 3:18-19

   B. 1 John 3:24

15. If your heart still condemns you, what comfort can you find in 1 John 3:19-20?

However firmly grounded the Christian's assurance is, his heart may sometimes need reassurance. . . . Sometimes the accusations of our "conscience" will be true accusations, and sometimes they will be false, inspired by "the accuser of our brethren" (Revelation 12:10). . . . Our conscience is by no means infallible; its condemnation may often be unjust. We can, therefore, appeal from our conscience to God who is greater and more knowledgeable. Indeed, he knows all things, including our secret motives and deepest resolves, and, it is implied, will be more merciful toward us than our own heart (John Stott, *The Epistles of John*, Inter-Varsity, pp. 145–46).

16. What do you think you will remember best from this chapter?

PRAYER TIME

Take prayer requests and then pray, using Popcorn Prayer. Close your prayer time by singing "Behold, What Manner of Love" (p. 100).

Five

The Joy of Overcoming Love
1 John 4

When our son John was sixteen, he went through a period of rebellion and was befriended by a group of boys who drank. My husband and I became stricter with John, changing his curfew. But he'd sneak out of his bedroom window after we were asleep. It was a terrible time for all of us. John was experiencing the consequences of sin, and my husband and I always feared the worst—a phone call saying there'd been an accident.... My sister Sally prayed and fasted with me that Satan's hold on John would be broken. "Greater is He that is in you, Dee," Sally said, "than the one who is in the world" (1 John 4:4).

My mentor, Shirley Ellis, reminded me of God's faithfulness. And she talked to me about the importance of showing John love, even though I was angry with his behavior. A beautiful word picture of the power of love occurs in Song of Songs 8:7 where we are told "Many waters cannot quench love; rivers cannot wash it away." The picture I had was of my surly teenage son throwing buckets of water on my love, and yet, being unable to quench it! And so as God persisted in loving me, I persisted in loving John. I played chess with him. I gave him backrubs. And I prayed and fasted for him.

John came back to God that year, coming to Him and to us in repentance one morning. Since that day ten years ago, John has walked closely with God, loving Him and serving Him.

"Beloved, let us love one another" (1 John 4:7). God's love is an overcoming love!

OPENING SONG
Sing "Beloved (1 John 4:7-8)" (p. 95).

WARMUP
Ask group members to finish this sentence: **When someone returns my unkindness with kindness, I feel. . . .**

Ask if anyone has been blessed by her secret sister—and how.

MEMORY VERSES

Beloved, let us love one another: for love is of God, and every one that loveth is born of God, and knoweth God. He that loveth not knoweth not God; for God is love (1 John 4:7-8, KJV).

SCRIPTURE STUDY
The Scripture study is divided into five days, for five personal quiet times with the Lord.

DAY 1 . . . .
She Discerns The Spirits
Peter describes our enemy the devil, as "a roaring lion" prowling around looking for someone to devour (1 Peter 5:8). "Be alert!" the apostle warns. The devil wants to rob us (and our children) of our joy and fruitfulness. And he is not only inspiring the cults and false teachers, but you can find him in schools, in movies, even on "Oprah." And the world is listening to him, making his books, movies, and music big business! Jesus tells us that the devil can disguise himself as an angel of light. How then are we to recognize him?

Read 1 John 4:1-6.
Circle or note how many times in this passage John uses the phrases "is from," "are from." "is not from," or "are not from." John wants us to recognize the source of everything we read, see, or hear.

48

1. John gives two distinguishing tests to discern the spirits. Describe them:

   A. 1 John 4:2-3

"Come in the flesh" refers to the Incarnation which means Jesus is God.

   B. 1 John 4:5-6

2. A speaker who possesses the Spirit of God or a speaker that possesses the spirit of the antichrist stimulates a predictable reaction from an audience that contains both unbelievers and believers. Describe a time when you have seen this happen (a classroom, observing a talk show audience, etc.).

John is saying here that we must be gentle and winsome when we present the message of God. However, even when we are gentle and winsome, rejection should not surprise us (1 John 3:13).

3. With the tests of 1 John 4:2, 5 in mind, give an example of a philosophy, book, or TV show that passes these tests and another that fails these tests.

   A. What example(s) can you give that shows the Spirit of God? How does it pass the above tests?

   B. What example(s) can you give that shows the spirit of the antichrist? How does it fail the above tests?

DAY 2
She Overcomes the Spirit of the Antichrist
When Satan waged a war for our son John, my husband and I joined forces with friends to pray fervently for him. When the

battle was fiercest, we clung to this promise: "He who is in you is greater than he who is in the world" (1 John 4:4).

Today you will discover ways to wage spiritual battle and overcome the spirit of the antichrist—not only in your own mind and heart, but in the minds and hearts of the children to whom God has entrusted you.

Read Ephesians 6:12-18.

4. Describe the struggle (v. 12). How have you seen this spiritual battle in your life?

How have you seen this in the lives of the children to whom God has entrusted you? If you are not a parent, how have you seen this in the lives of your friends, nieces, or nephews?

5. Describe our resources for the battle. Explain in practical terms how you could better use the resources found in each of the following passages.

A. Eph. 6:13-15

B. Eph. 6:16

C. Eph. 6:17

D. Eph. 6:18

Action Assignment. Choose one of the following actions and do it today or tomorrow! At your small group, you will be asked what you did.

A. Watch a secular TV program with a child. Ask him or her afterward: **What were the Christian values? What were the values that opposed Christ?**

B. Pray through Colossians 1:9-10 for a child you care about.

C. At dinner, bring out the *TV Guide* and discuss with your family what Christian or nonChristian themes are evident in some of the shows they have seen. When you've completed the Action Assignment, record what you did and any comments.

DAY 3
. . . .
She Overcomes with Love

When our daughter Sally was a seventh grader, an eighth grade girl chose her to be the target of her jokes. One night Sally tearfully told: "When I came into computer lab today, Amber tripped me! I sprawled all over the floor. She and her friends laughed hysterically."

After comforting my daughter (and resisting the urge to personally strangle Amber!), we talked about the kind of love that overcomes evil. Romans 12:19-21 says:

> Do not take revenge, my friends, but leave room for God's wrath, for it is written: It is mine to avenge; I will repay, says the Lord. One the contrary: If your enemy is hungry, feed him; If he is thirsty, give him something to drink. In doing this, you will heap burning coals on his head. Do not be overcome by evil, but overcome evil with good.

With a plan and all of my prayer support behind her, Sally entered the computer lab the next day and walked right up to Amber and said: "Amber, I saw your tennis scores in the paper. Good job!"

Sally came running home from school that night. Breathlessly, she said, "Mom! It worked! Amber blushed when I said that—and then, really meekly, she said: 'Thanks.' And later, when I passed her in the hall, she said: 'Hi, Sally.' "

The hardest time to love someone is when they don't deserve it. We certainly didn't deserve to have Jesus die for us—yet He did, and now He calls us to give the same kind of love to others.

Read 1 John 4:7-11.

6. What reason does John give us for showing overcoming love to one another?

Can you think of a time when you showed or were shown overcoming love? If so, share something about it.

The best translation of 1 John 4:8b is not "God is love," for that could lead you to the inaccurate idea that God is an abstraction. The Greek really says, "God as to His nature is love" (Kenneth Wuest, *Word Studies in the Greek New Testament,* Eerdmans, pp. 163–64).

7. Look up the words *atonement* and *propitiation*. What do you learn?

How did Jesus make it possible for God to be favorably disposed toward us?

8. What conclusion does John come to in verse 11?

Is there a child, neighbor, or relative to whom God is prompting you to show overcoming love? If so, whom? What will you do?

DAY 4
The Evidence of the Spirit
Everyone who has received Christ has received the fullness of the Spirit. We cannot see the Holy Spirit, but we can see evidence of Him at work in our lives. Likewise, others cannot see God, but they can see evidence of God in the love of believers.

Read 1 John 4:12-18.

9. What similar thought is repeated in verses 12 and 17?

   Have you experienced more of the presence of God when you
   have lived out His love? If so, share something about it.

John repeatedly emphasizes that if we have some fears concerning
the genuineness of our conversion, we can set those fears to rest
through living out God's love. I find this intriguing, because as an
evangelical, this theme is rarely emphasized. Instead, we are told,
(and this too is Scripturally sound) to rest in the grace of God. And
yet again and again John says that obedience leads to "confidence!" And "mature" love drives out fear.

11. According to the following verses, what kind of behavior will
    make us confident?

    A. 1 John 2:28

    B. 1 John 3:18-19

    C. 1 John 4:16-17

11. Judgment Day will be a day of shame and terror for the wick-
    ed. How should the child of God feel? Why? (1 John 4:16-18)

John Stott explains the phrase "as He is (i.e., Christ), so are we in
this world."

   Jesus is God's beloved Son, in whom He is well pleased; we
   too are God's children and the objects of His favour (*The
   Epistles of John*, Tyndale, p. 169).

DAY 5 . . . .
Mature Love Drives Out Hate

How do you react when a relative or friend hurts your feelings?
The most natural response in the world to pain is withdrawal. But
God does not call us to be *natural*, He calls us to be *supernatural*.

Read 1 John 4:19-21.

12. Why should we love? (v. 19)

What strong statements does John make? (v. 20)

13. Write the *natural* response in the following situations and then record the *supernatural* response.

A. You get along well with the other fifth floor employees—a new girl is hired who is a bit "irregular" and not well liked.

The *natural* response

The *supernatural* response

B. A good friend hurts your feelings.

The *natural* response

The *supernatural* response

C. Your son marries a girl you don't particularly like.

The *natural* response

The *supernatural* response

14. Is God speaking to you through this lesson? If so, how?

PRAYER TIME

Pray, using the last answer as a guide for Popcorn Prayer. Then close by singing "Beloved (1 John 4:7-8)" (p. 95).

Six

The Joy of Overcoming Faith

1 John 5

This year I led a women's Bible study made up primarily of beginners. In the first weeks, the women were inhibited about praying together. But then something happened.

During a study, a mother began to weep as she shared her frustrations about her disrespectful teenager. "She told me she hates me and she hopes I'll die!" Lynn wept. Sympathetically, the women next to her hugged her. We spontaneously surrounded her chair and began to pray for her:

"Father, please give Lynn wisdom with her daughter."

"Yes, Lord. And please melt Molly's heart."

"Lord, please have Lynn's husband intervene when Molly is disrespectful."

"Yes, Lord—I agree."

The next week Lynn came into the study brimming with news: "Last week, after you prayed," she said excitedly, "I asked Molly to take out the trash after supper. She ran up to her room and said, 'No! I'm not your slave!' My husband calmly followed her and brought her back down. Firmly he told her she was not to talk to me like that. Then he had her take out the trash. Molly and I were both stunned because he'd *never* intervened like that before. Suddenly I realized, 'That's because those women prayed!' "

That week the inhibitions to prayer came down. Women were willing to say simple sentences prayers—and to say, "I agree, Lord!" And we began to see things happen. Oh, the joy of overcoming faith!

John ends this letter much as he began it—we belong to a real God! This is no fairy tale! Jesus is real! The Spirit is real! And the woman who realizes this is plugged into a power that can overcome the world!

OPENING SONG
Sing "Behold, What Manner of Love" (p. 100) and "Rejoice in the Lord Always" (p. 99).

WARMUP
Briefly share an example of answered prayer from your life that had an impact on you. What did that cause you to believe about God?

MEMORY VERSES

I write these things to you who believe in the name of the Son of God so that you may know that you have eternal life. This is the confidence we have in approaching God: that if we ask anything according to His will, He hears us (1 John 5:13-14).

SCRIPTURE STUDY
The Scripture study is divided into five days, for five personal quiet times with the Lord.

DAY 1
Her Faith Is Not Burdensome because It Overcomes the World!
I've just returned from giving a retreat in the Seattle area. The women at that retreat loved the Lord deeply. It was evident in so many ways! They sang praises to Him with their whole hearts.

They loved each other—weeping with sisters in sorrow and surrounding them with prayer; laughing with sisters who were performing a crazy skit laden with spiritual truths; and listening to my messages with eager ears, wanting to go deeper into the Word of God and to live in obedience to Him. Why? Because obedience to His commands overcomes the world!

Read 1 John 5:1-5.
1. According to verse 1, what are two consequences of believing that Jesus is the Christ?

2. Why is it logical that if you love the father you love the child too?

Why is it logical that if you love God you obey His commands?

3. One of the reasons the commands of God are not burdensome to a believer is because they empower her to overcome the world. Review some of the commands in 1 John that can help you overcome the problems or sorrows of the world (1:7, 9; 2:15-17; 4:12).

Share personally and specifically how one of the above commands has given you victory and joy.

DAY 2
Her Faith Is Based on Reliable Evidence
Most people have a longing for spiritual reality—and that has led them in many directions. The late Paul Little has said that it is crucial to examine the object of our faith, for our faith is only as reliable as the object in which it is placed. For example, if a man believes with his whole heart that his faulty parachute will take him safely to the ground, he will still crash—for what matters is

not the sincerity of his faith, but the reliability of the object in which it is placed. How reliable an object is Jesus?

Read 1 John 5:6-10.

4. How did Jesus come by water at the beginning of His earthly ministry? What evidence was given then for trusting Him? (Matt. 3:13-17)

How did Jesus come by blood at the end of His earthly ministry? What evidence was given then for trusting Him? (List things such as fulfilled prophecies and supernatural events. A few examples are in Matt. 27:3-10, 50-54; 28:1-10.)

It is the historical evidences that lead a woman to trust Christ. Yet when she puts her trust in Christ, the Holy Spirit confirms in her heart that she was right to do so. In my life, I came to Christ because of the overwhelming evidence: the hundreds of fulfilled prophecies, the evidence for the Resurrection, the changed lives of the apostles. Yet the day I knelt and surrendered my life to Him, two things happened that I didn't expect: God took a burden from my back that I didn't even know I'd been carrying, and He took the blinders from my eyes that I didn't even know I'd been wearing. God's Spirit confirmed to me that Jesus truly was who He claimed to be — God!

5. Now John mentions this third testimony, that of the Holy Spirit, reminding us of Romans 8:16: "The Spirit Himself testifies with our spirit that we are God's children." After you put your trust in Christ, in what ways did God's Spirit confirm to you that you were right to do so?

Why is the person who refuses to believe not given further testimony?

DAY 3
. . . .

The Joy of Knowing We Have Eternal Life!

As a new believer I had a bumper sticker that said, "I'm bound for the promised land." A friend asked me what that meant, and I told her, "It means that I am confident of heaven." Her raised eyebrows caused me to explain. "I am confident, not because I feel that I am worthy—because I'm not. For years I completely ignored God and lived for myself. And even now, though I've given my life to Christ, I fail Him every day. I am still so unworthy. But I'm forgiven. Salvation is based on my trust in Christ's payment for my sin on the cross. That is why I know I have eternal life."

In your personal quiet time, sing praises for God's amazing grace. (Suggestions: "Behold, What Manner of Love" (p. 100), "Amazing Grace," and "And Can It Be?")

Read 1 John 5:11-13.

6. What black-and-white statement does John make in verse 12? What is one of the purposes of John's letter, according to verse 13?

   What does it mean to you that you can *know*—not *hope*—that you have eternal life?

John's letter reflects a balance that is often missing in both mainline and evangelical churches. Whereas mainline churches may fail to emphasize that we are saved by faith, evangelical churches may fail to emphasize that genuine faith results in a transformed life. If we do not obey God's Word, if we do not love our brother, if we are continually sinning—then we have reason to doubt that we have genuine saving faith. John tells us repeatedly that our confidence in our salvation will grow as we see these evidences in our life—not because they save us, but because they demonstrate that God's Spirit lives in us.

7. Do you see the following evidences in your life for saving faith? If so, share a specific:

A. 1 John 2:1

B. 1 John 2:3

C. 1 John 2:9-10

DAY 4 ....
The Joy of Knowing He Hears Us

In *What Happens When Women Pray,* Evelyn Christenson tells how God transformed eight gripers (the tired spiritual life chairwomen of her church!) into eight women who learned to pray together. The result? Their church was absolutely revitalized! Not only that, it was contagious, as sisters across America came to Mrs. Christenson's prayer seminars. When one woman was invited by her sister to a seminar, she thought: *A prayer seminar? What good will it do? I have prayed and prayed and it hasn't done any good.* She and her family were suffering from financial and health problems—and she doubted more prayer would help. But she went.

At that seminar, 1 John 5:14-15 changed her heart. "Up to that point," she said, "I had not asked for God's will—I could only see what I wanted to happen." But that day, as she stood with four Christian sisters, she prayed: "Lord, I want your perfect will for me and my family."

At that moment she felt the load lift. Nine months later she said: "I cannot begin to tell you of the peace I have in my heart. My husband's business debts are not all cleared up as yet, but God is moving. The burden is lifted. My health has improved tremendously." Her prayers, she now believes, went unanswered before because she had not asked God for His will.

Read 1 John 5:14-15.

8. What confidence can we have in approaching God?

What prerequisite is given in verse 14? What does this mean?

What other prerequisite is given in 1 John 3:22?

9. What is an earnest prayer desire of your heart? How might you apply the above prerequisites to this?

Read 1 John 5:16-17.

This is, perhaps, the most difficult passage in 1 John. The most convincing explanation I have heard of the "sin unto death" is made by John Stott who says, in the context of the whole letter, that sin is the rejection of Christ. Throughout the letter we are warned against counterfeits, those who claim to be brothers, but in reality have rejected Christ (*Epistles of John*, Tyndale, p. 190).

We cannot pray for them to be saved apart from Christ, but we can pray for genuine brothers and sisters who have sinned in other ways, and God will give them life.

DAY 5
Jesus Will Keep You, but Keep Yourselves from Idols!
A study of the Greek words translated *keep* in the closing passage of 1 John reveals the concept of *guard*. God will guard His children against Satan, who is prowling like a roaring lion, but we have a responsibility to guard our hearts from anything that would get between us and God. This requires diligence, just as an actual guard must not fall asleep on the job!

To begin your personal quiet time, sing "Behold, What Manner of Love" (p. 100).

Read 1 John 5:18-21.
10. Describe how the word *keep* is used in verse 18. How does this make you feel?

   Think back and remember a time when God kept you from the snares of Satan. What was the snare and how did God keep you?

11. What responsibility is given to us in verse 21?

   What are some of the "idols" that tend to get between you and God?

The word *keep* in verse 21 may have the connotation in the Greek of guarding through isolation. This is contrary to the way the world thinks, for the world encourages exposure. Those who "isolate" themselves from certain books, movies, sexual expressions, material pleasures . . . are labeled as "narrow." And yet here, God tells us to guard our hearts, to isolate ourselves from certain influences. It reminds me of the Titus 2 passage where women are told to be "keepers at home," or "guards over the hearts of their children." You can see this value in homeschoolers, or in believers who are embracing a simple lifestyle, in mothers who are careful about their children's choice of friends, or in individuals who have opted to live without TV. The world doesn't understand them and disparages them, but they are endeavoring to obey God in setting a guard over their hearts. God will not lead all of us in the same way—but we are all to seriously endeavor to "keep ourselves from idols"—from anything that would come between us and God.

12. How is God leading you to guard your heart? To guard the hearts of those in your care?

13. Look at the three "we knows" in 1 John 5:18-20. What do believers know? And how does this make them different from those in the world?

14. What has God impressed on your heart from this study or the discussion of 1 John 5?

PRAYER TIME

Pray, using Question #9 as a guide for Popcorn Prayer. Remember to ask for God's will and to make sure there is nothing between you and God when you pray. Close with "Father, I Adore You" (p. 93).

Seven

The Joy of Seeing
Our Children Walk in the Truth
2 John

Twenty years ago in Ohio, I had the joy of being used of God to lead a young mother of three small children to the Lord. Jesus turned Lee Petno's life around—and the change was so evident that her husband, upon meeting me, said, "Are you the one who is responsible for the wonderful change in my wife?"

I laughed and said, "No—Jesus did that!"

"Really!" he said, astonished. Soon after that he too put his trust in Christ.

Two years ago I flew back to Ohio for Lee's daughter's wedding. The wedding was distinctively Christian, with both the bride and groom expressing a heartfelt faith. At the reception, I visited with Lee's now grown sons and heard them express their passion for serving Christ. When I returned home I wrote Lee a letter that expressed a joy similar to that found in 2 John. How it thrilled my heart to see her and her husband continuing in the truth, and to see their children walking in the truth as well! What an affirmation of the power of the Spirit, to change lives from one generation to the next. And how I longed for her to continue loving God and guarding her heart and the hearts of those she was influencing against that which would pull them away from Christ's mighty power.

John writes to the elect lady, and commentators are divided on whether this is a woman who had been a leader in the early church, or whether this is a symbolic way of addressing a church. I am increasingly persuaded that it is the first — for that is the most natural way to interpret John's words. He also closes with greetings from her sister! But in either case, he is writing because he has met either some of her literal children or some of the children of that particular body and found them living wholeheartedly for Christ. It gave him great joy! And now he urges her to continue in love and in guarding her heart — for there is much antichrist propaganda around!

OPENING SONG
Sing "Rejoice in the Lord Always" (p. 99) and "This Is My Commandment" (p. 96).

WARMUP
Share a time when you felt joy because you saw your own children or the children of someone you loved walking in the truth. Why did it give you joy?

MEMORY VERSE

If anyone comes to you and does not bring this teaching, do not take him into your house or welcome him (2 John 10).

SCRIPTURE STUDY
The Scripture study is divided into five days, for five personal quiet times with the Lord.

DAY 1
The Joy of Finding Our Children Walking in the Truth
Proverbs tells us of the great joy that comes to the parent of a wise child (Prov. 10:1; 29:3). In my life, nothing has given me more joy than seeing our grown children walk in the truth. Women, whether they are biological mothers or spiritual mothers (and hopefully we are all the latter), experience great joy when they find their children walking in the truth.

Read through 2 John in its entirety; then read 2 John 1-4 again.

1. Note how many times John uses the word *truth* in this opening. When Jesus prayed for future believers in John 17:17, He prayed: "Sanctify them by the truth; Your word is truth." With this in mind, specifically imagine some ways that it would be evident that individuals had not just intellectually accepted the truth, but had welcomed it in their hearts.

2. What factors do you think contribute significantly to helping children walk in the truth?

My parents surrounded me with the Gospel and nestled me in their love for it. I often happened in on my father as he sat alone with the Bible, tears streaming down his cheeks at the beauty of some revelation. In our home, prayer was a natural response to problems and crises as well as good news and celebrations. My parents were verbal about their relationship with God, with each other, with us children, and with others (Gloria Gaither, *Today's Christian Woman,* Sept/Oct 1991, p. 48).

3. How did John pray for his spiritual children in verse 3?

Dr. James Dobson tells of a letter he received from his father which affected him profoundly. His father wrote:

I have observed that the greatest delusion is to suppose that our children will be devout Christians simply because their parents have been or that any of them will enter into life in any other way than through the valley of deep travail of prayer and faith. . . . But this prayer demands time, time that cannot be given if it is all signed and conscripted and laid on the altar of career ambition" (Rolf Zettersten, *Dr. Dobson: Turning Hearts Toward Home,* (Word, p. 93).

On-the-Spot Action Assignment. Spend some time in prayer for your biological or spiritual children. Pray through Colossians 1:9-12 and 2 John 3 for them.

DAY 2
Hold to Secret #1: Love One Another
If we want our children to walk in the truth, it is vital that we show them love. In Mike Yorkey and Greg Johnson's, *Faithful Parents, Faithful Kids* (Tyndale, p. 20), they continually stress: "Behavior is important, but relationship is the bull's-eye." If I have a good relationship with someone, if I know they love me, I want to please them. And yet it seems so many parents (and spiritual parents!) have lost sight of this. They fail to show their children love, to affirm them, to spend time with them—and still expect them to listen to hard truths.

Read 2 John 5-6.
4. John repeats Christ's command that we "walk in love." What does this mean?

If you are doing this guide in a small group, how might you better "walk in love" toward one another?

Action Assignment. Ask your children (or spiritual children) which of the following is their favorite way of receiving love.

1. Words of encouragement
2. Physical touch
3. Acts of service
4. Gifts
5. Spending time

Then, endeavor to love one of your children, this week, in his favorite way to be loved. What do you plan to do?

5. What is your favorite way of receiving love? (Be particularly alert to your secret sister's favorite way of receiving love!)

DAY 3 ....

Hold to Secret #2:
Watch out for Antichristian Propaganda!

In John's day, deceivers were coming to believers and offering a "new and improved" religion. Instead of presenting the simplicity of the Gospel, they had added to it, twisted it, and said it was better! The same telltale sign is evident in today's cults. Also, many religions claim to have God—but they do not want Christ. John says here that neither, therefore, do they have God.

Read 2 John 7-11.
6. Find the marks of a deceiver in verses 7 and 9.

   What strong statement does John make in verse 9 about the person who does not continue in the teachings of Christ?

Denying that Jesus came in the flesh was denying the incarnation, that Deity became man. They denied that Christ was God. John Stott says: "Many today want God without Jesus Christ. They say they believe in God, but see no necessity for Jesus. Or they want to bring non-Christian religions on to a level with Christianity, as alternative roads to God. . . . John refers sarcastically to their claim. They had indeed 'gone ahead.' They had advanced so far that they had left God behind them!" (*The Epistles of John,* Tyndale, p. 211)

7. It's popular today, as in John's day, to be religious—but not to embrace Jesus Christ. What warnings does John give to us in verses 8, 10-11?

In John's day, the practice of hospitality was so habitual that people seldom stayed in inns, and the inns that did exist were dirty and run-down. Therefore, missionaries almost always stayed in homes. John is telling believers that if they support false missionaries in this way, they are participating in their evil work. I do not think this passage means that we are to be rude to the occasional cult member who comes to our door, though we certainly should guard our hearts. Rudeness certainly won't win them—and neither will quarrels. When someone has been deceived (whether it is a cult member, a prodigal child, or an unbelieving coworker), arguments only heighten their defense. But love, kindness, and a humble testimony of Christ's power in our life may break down those walls.

Read 2 Timothy 2:23-26.
8. What principles are given here for discussions with those who do not accept the claims of Christ?

DAY 4

Antichristian Propaganda and the Mass Media

David Mains has pointed out that in John's day false teaching was limited to false missionaries—but today antichristian propaganda has multiplied through the mass media. John's warnings should sound loudly in our ears when we think about all the ways the mass media can come into our homes and influence us and our loved ones. About ten years ago I found myself wondering if there were any common variables among women who were walking in the truth and who had raised children who were walking in the truth. This led to a survey I did of 4,000 Christian women who came to my retreats. (The full results are in *The Lifestyles of Christian Women.*) One of my most significant discoveries was that women who were leading radically transformed Christian lives had this in common:

> They severely limited their time with TV and they spent that time instead, listening to Christian music, Christian radio, and reading the Scripture and Christian books. And from an early age, they helped their children to do likewise.

Review 2 John 4 and 7-11.
9. Do you see a connection between verse 4 and the warning in verses 7-11? In your own life? In the lives of the next generation? If so, share something about it.

David Mains sees a false religion sweeping North America and much of the world and dominating the mass media. He says: "This sinister force I'm describing rejects Christ totally and ridicules those who speak on His behalf. It befriends other religions, but uniquely HATES the Son of God and all He represents. . . . This religion preaches a morality that not only opposes biblical Christianity but attacks many traditional standards of morality. . . . This is not just secular humanism. That name is too neutral. What is it? It is the aggressive, blatant, powerful, growing end-time religion of the antichrist" ("The Religion of Antichrist," pamphlet published by The Chapel of the Air).

10. Have you made a conscious effort to limit the ways antichristian propaganda comes into your home? Or into your heart? If you have had some success, share what you have done with the group.

11. How might a mother decrease the antichristian propaganda that comes into her children's hearts and increase the truth they are exposed to?

By the time Billy Graham was ten, he'd memorized many passages of Scripture and all 107 articles in the Shorter Catechism. "We had Bible reading and prayer right after supper," his mother said. "We all got down on our knees and prayed, yes we did, sometimes from twenty to thirty minutes." Every Sunday afternoon Mrs. Graham would collect the children around the radio to listen to Charles Fuller's "Old Fashioned Revival Hour" (Marshall Frady, *Billy Graham*, Little, Brown, & Co., p. 48).

DAY 5
....
Maintaining Long-Distance Relationships
How do you maintain a friendship with a soulmate who moves across the country? With an adult child? John shows us the model of the New Testament:

1. Continued prayer
2. Continued letter writing (Or today—perhaps E-mail!)
3. Occasional visits, as the Lord permits

Obviously you cannot possibly carry out these three practices with everyone who is dear to you. But I have found it helpful to ask the Lord to guide me concerning with whom He wishes me to remain in close contact. With His guidance, and His help, I am endeavoring to remain close to all of my immediate family and a few long-distance friends.

On-the-Spot Action Assignment. As you are still before the Lord, to whom is He leading you to stay in contact? (Questions that I have found helpful are: Is my soul knit to her? Has she shown a desire to remain in touch with me? How are you leading, Lord?)

Read 2 John 12-13.
12. What does John tell the recipient of this letter in verse 12?

What is the value of face-to-face visits over letters?

Kenneth Wuest observes that the sight of people's faces appeals to one's heart and softens one's speech, and often our judgment of them is modified. He tells of how Dr. Dale of Birmingham looked with disfavor on Mr. Moody until he went to hear him. "He regarded him ever after with profound respect, and considered that he had a right to preach the Gospel, 'because he could never speak of a lost soul without tears in his eyes'" (*Word Studies in the New Testament,* Eerdmans, pp. 208-209).

71

13. Do you have some long-distance friends or family members who have endeavored to remain close to you? How have they done it and what has it meant to you?

14. What do you think you will remember from 2 John that will make a difference in your life?

Remind the group that next week you will be revealing your secret sisters. You may wish to plan a special luncheon or refreshments.

PRAYER TIME

Take prayer requests. Then pray using Popcorn Prayer. Close by singing "I Love You, Lord" (p. 101) and "This Is My Commandment" (p. 96).

Eight

The Joy of Hospitality

3 John

When my husband Steve was seeking a Christian medical practice, one of our visits took us to Iowa and a group of Mennonite doctors. The wife of one of the doctors invited me over to lunch on the spur of the moment. As I drove up to a compact ranch home, I wondered if I had scribbled down the wrong address (aren't doctors supposed to have big houses?). But it was Margie who opened the door, looking fresh and cheerful. Margie took my coat and I found myself talking easily as her eager questions coaxed me on. My eyes wandered over their living room. The grasscloth and pictures from Algeria reminded me that they had spent a few years in a mission hospital there. The room had warmth and character; its inexpensive simplicity was refreshing.

We sat down to a nicely set table and had Campbell's soup and canned peaches. Short notice didn't stop Margie from inviting me for lunch (it might have stopped me if I had been in her place!) Her priority was to meet me and develop a friendship, not to impress me.

Margie *did* impress me, but not in the way the world desires to impress. I was impressed by her Scriptural example of hospitality. She was not self-conscious about the simplicity of either her home or her lunch—there was not one word of apology. I doubt that it even occurred to her how differently I was being entertained than I had been on other job-hunting luncheons.

As we ate, Margie and I visited. It soon became evident that her hospitality was making an eternal difference in many lives. Not only was she hospitable to missionaries and those in ministry, but she had a thriving evangelistic study—more and more women from her block were coming, drawn to Margie, to her unintimidating yet warm home, and to Jesus Christ—the center of it all.

Our study closes with a very personal letter—to Gaius, who I believe exemplified many of the characteristics I saw in Margie. He loved to be hospitable to strangers, for the sake of Jesus, and visitors to his home came back to John and remarked, not on his impressive home, but on his love.

OPENING SONG
Sing "Beloved, (1 John 4:7-8)" (p. 95).

WARMUP
Share a time when someone's hospitality particularly ministered to you. What was it that ministered to you?

MEMORY VERSE

> Dear friend, you are faithful in what you are doing for the brothers, even though they are strangers to you (3 John 5).

SCRIPTURE STUDY
The Scripture study is divided into five days, for five personal quiet times with the Lord.

DAY 1
The Joy of Finding Faithfulness in Our Brethren
As in 2 John, John writes about the joy of finding "children" walking in the truth. Here he is referring to Gaius, who may have been one of his converts.

Read through 3 John in its entirety; then read 3 John 1-6 again.
1. Find a way that John encourages Gaius in each of the six opening verses.

What were some of the outstanding evidences of Gaius' spiritual health?

On-the-Spot Action Assignment. Encourage one another in your small group by sharing some of the outstanding evidences of one another's spiritual health. Go around the group and allow a few sentences of encouragement for each woman.

2. What ordinary or creative ways can you think of to imitate John's habit of encouraging your sisters and brothers in Christ spiritually?

DAY 2
Christian Hospitality

The way the world entertains should be very different from the way a Christian extends hospitality. The world desires to impress, the Christian should desire to minister. The world exclusively invites those who will be able to, in some way, repay. The Christian should be looking for ways, as Karen Mains says, "to be a catalyst for the miraculous."

As women, we are often the ones who decide whether or not and to whom our homes will be open. Here are just a few of the possibilities:

A. To encourage missionaries and ministry workers with a home-cooked meal and sharpening conversation.
B. To mentor younger women, helping them to love their husbands and children, through inviting them into our homes and allowing them to see a model — as Titus 2 instructs.
C. To provide a warm and loving atmosphere for one on one evangelism or an evangelistic Bible study.
D. To provide a temporary home for a woman in need of nurturing.
E. To provide a temporary or permanent home to a foster child or orphan.
F. To welcome someone to the community.

3. What are some ways you have used your home in Christian hospitality? What dreams do you have for extending your practice of Christian hospitality?

Read 3 John 5-6.
4. To whom was Gaius showing hospitality? Who would be some people you know who would fit into this category?

What do you think verse 6 means? What are some ways you could do this?

Read 3 John 7-8.
5. What do you learn about the recipients of Gaius' hospitality?

Why do you think they didn't receive help from unbelievers?

6. Read the following verses and write any added insight each gives you on Christian hospitality.

   A. Keep on loving each other as brothers. Do not forget to entertain strangers, for by so doing some people have entertained angels without knowing it (Heb. 13:1-2).

   B. Then Jesus said to his host, "When you give a luncheon or dinner, do not invite your friends, your brothers or relatives, or your rich neighbors; if you do, they may invite you back and so you will be repaid. But when you give a banquet, invite the poor, the crippled, the lame, the blind, and you will be blessed. Although they cannot repay you, you will be repaid at the resurrection of the righteous" (Luke 14:12-14).

Action Assignment. Invite a newcomer, a missionary, a woman who could use mentoring, or someone else that the Lord lays upon your heart over for a meal or dessert. Make your invitation today for sometime in the next week. Whom did you invite and why?

DAY 3
....
Be Hospitable to the Truth

In 2 John, we considered a broader application of the warning of being careful about welcoming antichristian propaganda into our homes by looking at the mass media. Here, in 3 John, we see the positive side of this warning. We are encouraged to be hospitable to the truth. We women can increase our family's exposure to the truth through our guests, and through the books, music, and programs we welcome into our homes.

7. If you were blessed to be raised in a home that was hospitable to the truth, share some ways your mother or father increased your exposure to the truth through:

   A. Guests (Do you remember a particular missionary or Christian who had an impact on you?)

   B. Music

   C. Books

8. What can you do to make your home more hospitable to the truth?

9. What blessings did the following people receive by being "hospitable to the truth"?

   A. The Shunammite woman (2 Kings 4:8-17)

B. The Philippian jailer (Acts 16:25-34)

What are some ways you or your family have been blessed by being hospitable to workers of the truth?

Virginia Hearns researched families of "well-turned out Christian children," looking for common variables. One commonality she found was that their homes were hospitable homes, frequently welcoming those who were in full-time Christian service. Their words and their lives helped the children of the host and hostess to grow immea-surably.

10. In Philippians 4:8, we're told to think about things that are noble, right, pure, lovely, admirable, excellent, and praiseworthy. List some specific books, radio programs, etc. that have helped you to do that. Share your list with your small group.

DAY 4 ....
The Real Reason for Inhospitality
Scripture has the power to change lives — if we are tender-hearted and willing to obey. Abbey is just such a woman. In response to my guide, *The Joy of Hospitality,* Abbey wrote:

> I had the usual excuses for not practicing hospitality — my house wasn't nice enough, I wasn't a good enough cook, I didn't have enough money . . . but your study stripped away my excuses and revealed the real reason for my inhospitality: a lack of concern for the needs of others. For Scripture showed me that the heart of hospitality is showing love. When I started thinking about the needs of others and stopped worrying about how impressed they'd be with me or my house, I began to reach out. Now, these are the kind of things I'm doing regularly: having newcomers to the church

over for popcorn on Sunday nights; picking up the son of a single mom when we go camping; and having our unsaved neighbors over for dessert while we draw them out with caring questions about their lives. These simple acts of obedience mean so much to them — and their joy wells up and makes our joy complete!

Review 3 John 5-8. Then read 3 John 9-10.
11. What three acts of inhospitality does John list about Diotrephes in this passage?

According to verse 9, what was his motive?

12. What are some of the typical reasons that people give to others or to themselves for failing to welcome those who need welcoming? What tends to be the real reason for inhospitality?

13. Who are some people in your life who need welcoming? Who are some people in your life who fit John's description in verses 7-8?

When you think about the people in the above two categories, what, if anything, is keeping you from encouraging or welcoming them into your home?

How do you think God would have you overcome these obstacles?

DAY 5 ....
Our Actions Reveal If God Is Alive and Well in Us!
John closes this letter with a familiar theme. If God really lives in you, you will do what is good. If your life is habitually evil (like the life of Diotrephes), then you have not seen God.

Read 3 John 11-13.

14. What does John say about Demetrius? How does he demonstrate one side of the principle in verse 11?

15. As a review of this principle, what point does John make in each of the following passages?

    A. 1 John 1:5-6

    B. 1 John 2:3-6

    C. 1 John 2:9-11

    D. 1 John 3:14-15

    E. 1 John 3:16-20

    F. 1 John 4:19-21

    G. 2 John 9

16. List two specific truths that God has impressed upon your heart from the letters of John.

    How are these truths making a difference in your life? (Be specific.)

PRAYER TIME

Use your answers to the last question as a guide for conversational prayer. Then close by singing "Behold What Matter of Love" (p. 100).

Leader's Helps

YOUR ROLE:

A FACILITATOR FOR THE HOLY SPIRIT
AND AN ENCOURAGER

A FACILITATOR FOR THE HOLY SPIRIT

People remember best what they articulate themselves, so your role is to encourage discussion and keep it on track. Here are some things you can do to help:

1. Ask questions and allow silences until someone speaks up. If the silence seems interminable, rephrase the question, but don't answer it yourself!
2. Direct the group members to look in the Scripture for their answers. For example, ask: "How can you see John's excitement in verse 1?"
3. Place chairs in as small a circle as possible. Space inhibits sharing.
4. Deal with the monopolizer:
   A. Pray not only for her control, but that you can help find ways to make her feel valued—for excessive talking often springs from deep emotional needs.
   B. Wait for her to take a breath and gently say: "Thanks, could we hear from someone else?"
   C. Go around the room with a question.
   D. Set down some ground rules at the beginning of the session. You can tell the group that you would like to hear from each person at least three times. So after they've spoken three times, they should give other group members a chance. You can even make a game of it and distribute pennies "to spend."
   E. Take the monopolizer aside and say: "You and I both share easily, but we have some women who are shy. How do you think we could help them to share more?"

5. The Action Assignments and memory work will be used mightily in your group members' lives. If they aren't doing these exercises, call a few from the group and ask them to be good examples with you. Soon the others will follow!

AN ENCOURAGER

Most women who drop out of a group do so not because the study is too challenging, but because they don't feel valued. As a leader, these are some of the things you can do to help each woman feel valued:

1. Greet each woman warmly when she walks in the door. This meeting should be the high point of her week!
2. Affirm answers when you can genuinely do so: "Good insight! Great! Thank you!" And always affirm nonverbally with your eyes, a smile, a nod.
3. If a woman gives a wrong or off-the-wall answer, be careful not to crush her. You can still affirm her by saying: "That's interesting—What does someone else think?" If you feel her response must be corrected, someone in the group will probably do it. If they don't, space your correction so it doesn't immediately follow her response and is not obviously directed at her.
4. If this is an interdenominational group, set this ground rule: No one is to speak unfavorably of another denomination.
5. Send notes to absentees and postcards to the faithful in appreciation.
6. Don't skimp on the prayer time. Women's emotional and spiritual needs are met during the prayer time, so allot one third of your time for that.

Leader's Helps for Chapter 1
The Joy of the Fellowship Circle

Distribute the guides ahead of time and assign Chapter 1.

IMPORTANT. Show the women where I, II, and III John are in the Bible. Some non-Christians and young Christians have tried to do this study using the Gospel of John, not knowing that John also wrote letters. They were hopelessly confused!

I have found it helpful to occasionally call on the shy people when it seems they might have something to share but need a little encouragement to share it. Tell them that if you do that and they don't have anything to share, to simply toss the ball to someone else by saying, "I don't know—Linda, what do you think?" If they form this habit in the beginning, you will have a richly interactive group instead of just hearing from the few who are comfortable sharing in groups.

OPTIONAL DISCUSSION QUESTIONS
Circle the following questions to skip in discussion if you are having trouble completing the chapter in your allotted time: #13, #16.

WARM UP
Bring name tags and write the women's first names in large letters. Read the first two paragraphs in the opening aloud—and then encourage the women to think back to their childhood. If they can't remember any thoughts about God, then they may share an early awareness. Tell them it doesn't have to be profound.

SCRIPTURE STUDY
Helps for Specific Questions

Reread the quote from Barclay and the following paragraph before you ask Question #1.

Question #3. Remember the height from which you've fallen. Repent. Do the things you did at first.

Question #6. Take time with this. Be alert to facial expressions. The shy ones might have something to share but need a little encouragement from you. ("Judy, you looked like you might have something to share.") You might share an answer to prayer for God's help in a difficult time to prime the pump for more sharing.

Question #16A. Ask them: **What makes you feel welcome when you come to this group? What would be some contemporary applications of "a holy kiss?"**

Question #16C. Help them visualize deep, dark water. Sometimes we don't even know the motives or desires at the bottom of our own hearts, for Jeremiah tells us we have deceptive hearts. But an understanding friend with caring questions can help us to see through to the bottom.

Leader's Helps for Chapter 2

The Joy of Walking in the Light

Write or call those who came last week and let them know you were glad they came!

OPTIONAL DISCUSSION QUESTIONS
Circle the following questions to skip in discussion if you have a group that has trouble finishing on time: #6, #13, #14.

WARMUP
Since the opening shared an example of God speaking through His still, small voice, you might share an example of God speaking to you through His Word to pave the way for varied sharing.

SCRIPTURE STUDY
Helps for Specific Questions
Question #2A. Light gives confidence.

Question #2B. Light gives guidance.

Question #10. Help them visualize a legal scene, with God as the Judge, Satan as our adversary, and Jesus as our Advocate. If you have those who are unfamiliar with the Gospel, explain how Jesus is our atoning sacrifice and how we need to trust Him.

Question #14. If time permits, go around with this question. You might begin and model vulnerability and brevity.

PRAYER TIME
Ahead of time, call three women who would be comfortable demonstrating Popcorn Prayer. Have them pray for three different subjects (each other). Emphasize that they model brevity by saying, "I agree," or "Yes, Lord."

The Joy That Will Not Pass Away

OPTIONAL DISCUSSION QUESTIONS
Circle the following questions to skip in discussion if you have a group that has trouble finishing on time: #7, #15.

SCRIPTURE STUDY
Helps for Specific Questions
Question #8. Kenneth Wuest (*Word Studies in the New Testament,* Eerdmans, p. 128) explains that the dominant sense of the last hour or last days in the New Testament means "a critical season." It is ushered in by antichrists, or those who propose to do the work of Christ but are false teachers. It culminates with the appearance of the Antichrist, one who will pretend to be the Messiah.

On-the-Spot Action Assignment. In the exchange of "secret sisters," give freedom to the women who don't wish to participate. If a group member's schedule is such that she knows she won't be able to participate, it's better to pass this time. But also stress that this shouldn't take much time or money—but simply be a fun way of showing love. Also, as a leader, spend some time in prayer before this assignment, asking God to pair up women according to His knowledge of them.

Leader's Helps for Chapter 4
The Joy of Calvary Love

OPTIONAL DISCUSSION QUESTIONS
Circle the following questions to skip in discussion if you have a
group that has trouble finishing on time: #3, #12.

SCRIPTURE STUDY
Helps for Specific Questions
Question #8. Take some time with this question, probing group
members with questions like: **What makes you feel envious?
How does envy make you feel? Have you had any success in
conquering envy? What helped?** In discussing depression, make
sure that your group doesn't conclude that depression is always a
result of disobedience, but simply that it could be.

Leader's Helps for Chapter 5
The Joy of Overcoming Love

OPTIONAL DISCUSSION QUESTIONS
Circle the following questions to skip in discussion if you have a group that has trouble finishing on time: #4, #5.

SCRIPTURE STUDY
Helps for Specific Questions
Question #8. Atonement and *propitiation* are rich words which picture satisfying the just demands of a holy God. If you have some in your group who may not understand why Christ had to die for our sins, this is an opportunity to clarify this central truth.

Leader's Helps for Chapter 6
The Joy of Overcoming Faith

OPTIONAL DISCUSSION QUESTIONS

Circle the following questions to skip in discussion if you have a group that has trouble finishing on time: #7, #9 (if this is a beginning group); #4 (if this is an intermediate group).

SCRIPTURE STUDY
Help for Specific Questions

Question #12. This would be a good question to go around the room with, giving women the freedom to pass.

Leader's Helps for Chapter 7

The Joy of Seeing
Our Children Walk in the Truth

OPTIONAL DISCUSSION QUESTIONS
Circle the following questions to skip in discussion if you have a group that has trouble finishing on time: #3, #4, #12.

SCRIPTURE STUDY
Help for Specific Questions
Question #9. Some questions might come in regard to verse 8. John Stott says: "The thought is not of their winning or losing their salvation (which is a free gift), but their reward for faithful service. The metaphor seems to be taken from the payment of labour, since reward (*misthos*) is a workman's wage" (*The Epistles of John*, IVP, p. 210). Like the workman who may become slack as the day goes on, John is fearful that believers may become slack, lose their guard, and receive less than a full day's pay.

Question #11. See if anyone has come up with a specific, workable plan for TV or secular music. The women whom I surveyed had done some of the following: coupons; no TV on weeknights; watching only shows recorded on the VCR; insisting on an hour of reading before the TV was turned on; or allowing only family-oriented or educational channels.

Leader's Helps for Chapter 8
The Joy of Hospitality

OPTIONAL DISCUSSION QUESTIONS
Circle the following questions to skip in discussion if you have a group that has trouble finishing on time: #6, #9, #10, #15.

SCRIPTURE STUDY
Question #11. This lesson is concentrating on hospitality, but another application has to do with church politics. If this group is a church study and you have an active women's ministry, you may want to ask for applications to this situation.

Question #12. To increase response, you can turn this question around and ask: **When have been some times in your life when you needed welcoming?** If you have anyone in your group who has moved recently or been in full-time Christian service, ask to hear from her.

Question #16. Go around the room with this question and have women take notes for prayer.

MEMORY VERSES

Chapter 1
We proclaim to you what we have seen and heard, so that you also may have fellowship with us. And our fellowship is with the Father and with His Son, Jesus Christ. We write this to make our joy complete (1 John 1:3-4).

Chapter 2
But if we walk in the light, as He is in the light, we have fellowship with one another, and the blood of Jesus, His Son, purifies us from all sin (1 John 1:7).

Chapter 3
The world and its desires pass away, but the man who does the will of God lives forever (1 John 2:17).

Chapter 4
This is how we know what love is: Jesus Christ laid down His life for us. And we ought to lay down our lives for our brothers (1 John 3:16).

Chapter 5
Beloved, let us love one another: for love is of God, and every one that loveth is born of God, and knoweth God. He that loveth not knoweth not God; for God is love (1 John 4:7-8, KJV).

Chapter 6
I write these things to you who believe in the name of the Son of God so that you may know that you have eternal life. This is the confidence we have in approaching God: that if we ask anything according to His will, He hears us (1 John 5:13-14).

Chapter 7
If anyone comes to you and does not bring this teaching, do not take him into your house or welcome him (2 John 10).

Chapter 8
Dear friend, you are faithful in what you are doing for the brothers, even though they are strangers to you (John 5).

Music

Closing with a song helps people leave a small group meeting with their focus on Jesus. Music Minister John Haines makes the following suggestions for a successful song time.

1. Teach the song the first time. Be sure you know it. If you cannot do this, delegate it to someone who can. Even if it is a familiar chorus to many, teach it the first time—for there will be those who don't know it.

2. Sing the song in a relatively low key.

Father, I Adore You

Terrye Coelho

* opt. ROUND

1. Fa - ther,
2. Je - sus, I a - dore you, lay my life be -
3. Spir - it,

fore you, how I love you.

* After every 2 measures, new group enters at ①

The Wonder of It All

Words and Music by
George Beverly Shea

1. There's the won-der of sun-set at eve-ning, The won-der as sun-rise I see; But the won-der of won-ders that thrills my soul Is the won-der that God loves me.

2. There's the won-der of spring-time and har-vest, The sky, the stars, the sun; But the won-der of won-ders that thrills my soul Is a won-der that's on-ly be-gun.

Refrain

O, the won-der of it all! The won-der of it all! Just to think that God loves me. O, the won-der of it all! The won-der of it all! Just to think that God loves me.

Beloved (1 John 4:7-8)

Dennis Ryder

Be - lov - ed,— let us love— one an - oth - er,— for love is of God, and ev - 'ry - one that lov - eth is born of God,— and know - eth God.— He that lov - eth not know - eth not God,— for God is love.— Be - lov - ed,— let us love— one an - oth - er, First John four: sev - en and eight.—

This Is My Commandment

Author Unknown

This is my com-mand-ment that you love one an-oth-er, that your joy may be full.

If We Walk in the Light

Author Unknown

Rejoice in the Lord Always

Words and Music by
Evelyn Tarner

Behold, What Manner of Love

I John 3:1

Patricia Van Tine

Be - hold, what man - ner of love the Fa - ther has giv - en un - to us.___ Be - hold, what man - ner of love the Fa - ther has giv - en un - to us, that we___ should be called the chil - dren of God, that we___ should be called the chil - dren of God.___

I Love You, Lord

Text and Music: Laurie Klein
arranged by Eugene Thomas

I love You, Lord,— and I lift my voice— to wor - ship You. O my soul, re - joice! Take joy, my King,— in— what You hear:— may it be a sweet, sweet— sound in— Your ear.

Prayers and Praises

_____

_____

_____

_____

_____

_____

_____

_____

_____

_____

_____

_____

_____

_____

Prayers and Praises

_____

_____

_____

_____

_____

_____

_____

_____

_____

_____

_____

_____

_____

Prayers and Praises

Prayers and Praises

_____

_____

_____

_____

_____

_____

_____

_____

_____

_____

_____

_____

_____

Prayers and Praises

Prayers and Praises

_____

_____

_____

_____

_____

_____

_____

_____

_____

_____

_____

_____

_____

_____

Prayers and Praises

Prayers and Praises

_____

_____

_____

_____

_____

_____

_____

_____

_____

_____

_____

_____

_____

_____

Prayers and Praises

_____

_____

_____

_____

_____

_____

_____

_____

_____

_____

_____

_____

_____

_____

Prayers and Praises

_____

_____

_____

_____

_____

_____

_____

_____

_____

_____

_____

_____

_____

_____